THE BLACK WATCH

Aldershot 1913. Orders of Dress.

Front Cover: Drummer Boy Haxton and Drum Major Hutton, *c*.1905.

Back Cover: The Black Watch is granted the Freedom of Perth, July 1947. The Colonel-in-Chief inspects men of the Regiment accompanied by Lieutenant Colonel B.C. Bradford.

THE BLACK WATCH

THE BLACK WATCH PHOTOGRAPHIC ARCHIVE

TEMPUS

First published 2000
Copyright © The Black Watch Regimental Trustees, 2000

Tempus Publishing Limited
The Mill, Brimscombe Port,
Stroud, Gloucestershire, GL5 2QG

ISBN 0 7524 1763 0

Typesetting and origination by
Tempus Publishing Limited
Printed in Great Britain by
Midway Clark Printing, Wiltshire

Pipe Major Small takes centre stage during the Farewell Parade on the handover of Hong Kong, June 1997.

Contents

Recruits visiting Aberfeldy, the birthplace of the Regiment.

Sergeants of the 2nd Battalion picnic in the Khyber Pass, 1906.

Introduction

This collection of photographs is not intended to be a history of The Black Watch but rather a selection of pictures in chronological sequence. It starts in 1852 with the earliest extant photograph of the regiment. By then, The Black Watch had been in existence for a little over one hundred years since the day it first paraded as a regiment on the banks of the Tay in 1740. While the epics of that first century are outside the scope of this volume, I believe there are two specific points which might help those unfamiliar with the early history of The Black Watch to place this later photographic era into context. The fact that The Black Watch was originally raised as Independent Companies to police the Highlands during the turbulent times of Jacobite unrest will be of interest when viewing photographs of very similar duties being carried out by the Regiment in such places as Palestine, Kenya, Cyprus and Northern Ireland. It might also be helpful to explain why, in the first section of the book up to 1881, two rather different regiments are depicted – one a kilted regiment, the 42nd Royal Highlanders, and the other an apparently English line regiment, the 73rd. The gallant performance of the Regiment during the war with France in North America led to a second battalion of the 42nd Royal Highlanders, as the Regiment was then known, being raised. Later, it was to become a separate regiment in its own right being numbered the 73rd and was to serve with distinction in India. During the period of the Napoleonic Wars the regiment ceased to be kilted but, later in the century, took the title of the 'Perthshire' Regiment. When the Army Reforms of 1881 joined pairs of Regiments together, the 42nd and 73rd were reunited to become the 1st and 2nd Battalions of The Black Watch.

The photographs have been selected to give as wide a coverage as possible of the Regiment's activities both in peace and war. It is, however, restricted at times by the availability of photographs, particularly during the earlier years and during periods of active service. An effort has been made to maintain a balance between the cover given to different battalions of the Regiment. Despite the many hundreds of photographs to choose from, this has not been an easy task for some battalions kept comprehensive photographic albums, while those of others have not survived or were less conscientiously maintained. Thus the 6th Battalion during the First World War and 2nd and 5th Battalions during the Second may appear over-represented but this is only due to lack of suitable material from the others. Inevitably, the number of photographs available to choose from increases with the passage of time. Some of them have appeared previously in the pages of the Regimental journal, *The Red Hackle*, but the majority have never been reproduced before and, for conservation reasons, are held in the Regimental Archives, unavailable for view by the general public.

Essentially, this is a photographic book entirely devoted to Black Watch soldiers and events in the life of the Regiment. The captions are subsidiary and are intended to place the pictures in context with one another, providing details of circumstances, dates and, where known, of individual identities. As many Regimental heroes and characters as possible are portrayed but it has only been practical to give the briefest of resumés of their careers.

I hope that the book conveys throughout a sense of the family spirit of The Black Watch both in terms of brothers-in-arms drawn mainly from one specific corner of Scotland, and also in the continuity of families serving in the Regiment generation after generation. It is this which has given such a great source of tenacity during battles of the past and continues to provide such strong cohesion within the Regiment to-day.

Stephen Lindsay
Regimental Secretary
The Black Watch (RHR)

Acknowledgements

The great majority of photographs in this volume are held in The Black Watch Regimental Archive in Balhousie Castle, Perth, and are reproduced with the permission of the Regimental Trustees.

Thanks are also due to D.C. Thompson & Co. Ltd, *The Perthshire Advertiser*, Louis Flood and Allan Walker for their agreement to the reproduction of photographs of which the Trustees do not hold the copyright.

Special thanks must also go to the Regimental Archivist, Thomas B. Smyth, who not only researched the identity of many of the individuals depicted in this book, but also took great trouble in checking the historical accuracy of the captions.

One
From 1852 to 1881

A group of Black Watch heroes of the Crimean War photographed at Dover in 1856 by command of Queen Victoria. They are Piper Muir, Privates Glen and Mackenzie and Colour Sergeant Gardner. Two years later Colour Sergeant Gardner was to be awarded the Victoria Cross for his conspicuous and gallant conduct in saving the life of his commanding officer who had been knocked from his horse and was being attacked by three rebels during the Indian Mutiny.

This is the earliest photograph of the 42nd Highlanders, dated 1852. It shows the Light Company of the Regiment in The Citadel, Halifax, Nova Scotia. Colour Sergeant Alexander McGregor has just handed the orders for the return to Scotland to the Company Commander, Captain Henry Drummond. He is reading them to the two officers, Lieutenants John Wedderburn and, on the right, John McLeod (later Lieutenant General Sir John McLeod, Colonel of The Regiment between 1907 and 1914). The piper in the centre is John MacDonald. The figure leaning on his musket to the left is Charles Christie who was drowned in the Ganges during the Indian Mutiny.

After taking part in suppressing the Indian Mutiny, the 42nd was stationed in India from 1859 to 1867. This photograph taken in Bareilly shows the various orders of dress. Notice that the piper and bandsman are both wearing Royal Stewart tartan. This was often referred to as the 'Music Tartan' and had been worn by the pipers since the early days of the Regiment. It was only worn intermittently by the Military Band for at other times it wore the Regimental tartan.

This superb figure is Drum Major Thomas Bosanquet of the 73rd Regiment photographed around 1862 when he had received the Good Conduct Medal. Originally raised as a 2nd Battalion of the 42nd Royal Highlanders in 1779, the 73rd became a regiment in its own right in 1786. Although it ceased to wear the kilt in 1809, it did become the 'Perthshire' Regiment in 1862 and, in the 1881 Army Reforms, was reunited with the 42nd as the 2nd Battalion The Black Watch (Royal Highlanders).

The Band of the 73rd pose in relaxed mode for the camera in Plymouth in 1862. The fact that Private Segrave (right rear) is blocking his ears indicates that some musical quality may have been missing! Unlike the remainder of the group the fiddler in mufti beside Bandboys Bartlett and Mayhew is unidentified. He is likely to have been a civilian music instructor or possibly even an Italian busker.

Left: The first member of the Regiment to receive the Victoria Cross was Lieutenant Francis Farquharson. He was awarded it for conspicuous bravery during the Indian Mutiny when he led some of his company to storm a two gun bastion at Lucknow on 9 March 1858. He was to be severely wounded the following day. This photograph was taken some five years later. He was promoted Major in 1874 and served in the Ashanti Campaign but died the following year.

Right: This picture shows the khaki uniform worn by the 42nd in 1874 for the Campaign in Ashanti, the modern-day Ghana. In that climate the kilt would have been totally inappropriate. The khaki uniform is seen here worn by Lieutenant Colonel Sir Francis Cunningham Scott, younger of Malleny. He later commanded the Ashanti Expedition of 1895-1896 as a Major General.

Following page, top: In 1859 a number of volunteer units were raised throughout the country. Amongst these was the 1st Forfarshire Rifle Volunteers. These two pictures show No.1 Company in camp at Monifieth, near Dundee. The tunics of the three officers would be scarlet, a change made from the original dark grey uniform in 1862. In the right hand picture Sergeant Major Souter has a young batman, perhaps his son, polishing his boots for him. In 1908 these Volunteers were to become the 4th Battalion The Black Watch (Territorial Force).

It was not until 1881 that permanent home depots were allocated to regiments. Prior to that depot companies were normally located with their regiment while it was in a home station. When it was abroad these depot companies moved between garrisons. While the 42nd was in India in 1867 the Depot is seen paraded here in Stirling Castle. The pipers and musicians are in front and it will be seen that many of these are bandboys. The officers on the right of the picture are Captain Francis Cunningham Scott wearing trews and Lieutenant George Moore who was wounded seven years later during the Ashanti Campaign as were two other officers on this parade, less easily identified.

This photograph of the Band of the 42nd was taken at Simla, an Indian hill station, in 1864 and at much the same period as that of the 73rd Band on page 11. Notice should be taken of the circular Star of the Thistle cap badges on the rather unbecoming 'pork pie' hats. This badge was in use for only a short period. Other interesting features on the accoutrements are the absence of St Andrew in the centre of the plaid brooches and of badges on the piper's cross belt. He, it will be seen, wears the more traditional bonnet.

In 1881 the 73rd returned home from India and were stationed in Portsmouth. On 23 February the Regiment was inspected by HSH Prince Edward of Saxe Weimar. The large arena marked out for the parade on Southsea Common is visible behind the Regiment. Rumour was already rife that it was soon to become a Highland regiment again and this may well have been the last occasion on which it formally paraded as the 73rd.

Two

From 1881 to 1899

The 1881 Cardwell Reforms amalgamated pairs of regiments so that one battalion would normally serve abroad while the other would be stationed at home. The 42nd became the 1st Battalion, The Black Watch (Royal Highlanders) in this reorganization and it left for Egypt the following year, remaining abroad throughout this period. The 73rd became the 2nd Battalion and continued to serve in Portsmouth. The photograph shows men of the 1st Battalion grouped around the Sphinx during a visit to the Pyramids.

At dawn on 13 September 1882 the 1st Battalion, as part of the Highland Brigade, stormed the strongly entrenched position of the numerically superior Egyptian Army at Tel-el-Kebir. It was a stunning victory and earned the Regiment another battle honour. A group of men from the Battalion (with a few others) are pictured visiting the Egyptian position some time after the battle.

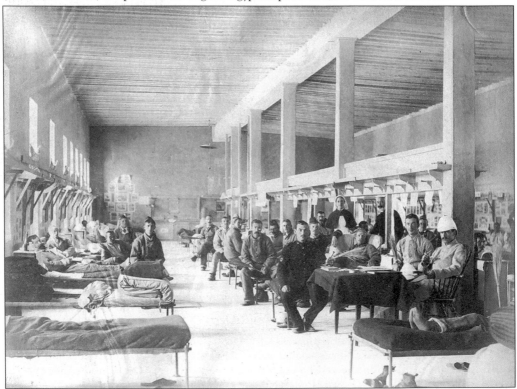

Battles are not won without casualties. Tel-el-Kebir was no exception but fortunately those of the Regiment were relatively few. Thirteen all ranks lost their lives while five officers, three sergeants and thirty-one rank and file were wounded. They are seen here in hospital in Egypt.

One of the Regiment's early Chelsea Pensioners was Private John McKay. This studio portrait is dated 1882 when he was ninety-seven years old. Born at Lairg, Sutherland, he was a veteran of the Napoleonic Wars and had been wounded both at the capture of Badajoz in 1812 and at Waterloo in 1815.

The formation of a square had been the standard practice by infantry to repel attacks by cavalry. Squares were again used against the Mahdi's fanatical tribesmen when the 1st Battalion fought at the battles of El Teb and Tamai in the Sudan in 1884. Here the Battalion is seen in square formation during training but wearing feather bonnets rather than the pith helmets worn during that campaign.

Sport has always played a large part in the life of the Regiment – and it still does. Not only is it a satisfying way of maintaining physical fitness but it also plays an important role in developing team spirit and Regimental pride. The four pictures on these two pages show a variety of the sports participated in. There are eleven men in this stalwart tug of war team for it was only later that eight men became the accepted strength for competitions.

Polo was always popular amongst the officers. This is the team of the 73rd at Lucknow in their last year as a separate regiment. Lieutenant Archibald Carthew-Yorstoun, seated in the dark shirt went on to command the 2nd Battalion during the Boer War but was wounded at Paardeberg in February 1900. Lieutenant Ernest Willshire, seated at the front centre, took over command from him but died of wounds received at Retief's Nek in July that same year. Lieutenant Burton, seated between these two, commanded the 1st Battalion between 1906-1910. Both he and Carthew-Yorstoun served during the First World War while, Carthew-Yorstoun had a son in the Second World War, a grandson in the Korean War and a great-grandson who also served in the Regiment.

Between August and November 1895 the Regiment had the privilege of providing the Guard for HM Queen Victoria while she was in residence at Balmoral. The trophies are evidence that the officers made the most of the opportunities on Deeside at that time of year. The commander of the Guard, the officer in the centre equipped for fishing, is Captain Thomas Berkeley. He was to be wounded twice during the Boer War and to be killed in action during the First World War. The subalterns are Colin MacRae (later Sir Colin MacRae of Feoirlinn KT), the piper and John Hamilton who commanded the 1st Battalion in 1916 and again after the war in 1919.

Unofficially the 1st Battalion continued to use its previous number, 42 as emblazoned on the strips of the football team in 1899. They are pictured with the Durand Cup, the All India Football Trophy. As this was the third consecutive year in which they had won the competition, the team were allowed to retain the cup which is now in the Regimental Museum. Standing are Privates Smith, Johnston, Forrest and Sutherland (the trainer). Seated are Lance Corporal Hunter with Privates Scott, Watson and McLatchie and, in front, Aitken, McNaughton, Jamieson, Campbell and Young.

The 1st Battalion had four very eventful years in Egypt between 1882 and 1886, starting with the fight against the Egyptian Army at Tel-el-Kebir and then the campaign against the Mahdi. It ended with the Nile Expedition attempting to rescue General Gordon in Khartoum, involving the Battalion in a successful charge at the battle of Kirbekan. It then moved to Malta where it is here seen drawn up on parade. There is no obvious reason why the officers should be wearing different orders of dress from each other and from the remainder of the Battalion. The pioneers are clearly identifiable positioned on the nearside of the parade in front of the Pipes and Drums. This was their usual position on formal parades.

From Malta the 1st Battalion was posted in 1889 to Gibraltar for three years. Training obviously included building such substantial constructions as this bridge. At this time spats are being worn under the trews by all ranks but later this was confined to the officers. Note the pipers positioned at each of the uprights.

In 1881 the Regimental Depot was permanently established in Queens Barracks, Perth. This had been built in 1794 and was named after the first regiment to occupy it – the 4th (Queens Own) Dragoons. It was to become the home of the Regiment for the next eighty years – but the connection with the Barracks went back even longer for the 42nd had shared the accommodation with the 79th (Camerons) as early as 1830. Here a party of senior non-commissioned officers is ready to leave the barracks on a horse-drawn vehicle.

From Gibraltar, the 1st Battalion moved via Egypt to be split between Mauritius and South Africa. This photograph shows members of the Sergeants Mess in a wide variety of differing orders of dress. It would have been a colourful array with the white shell jackets, scarlet tunics, blue patrols and the green doublet worn by the Pipe Major. It is the first photograph of the Regiment which shows a bicycle.

The photographs on these two pages show various specialist sections within battalions. Here the Colour Sergeants are grouped around the Colours of the 1st Battalion, the two escorts to the Colours having their bayonets fixed. These colours were presented to the 42nd by HRH The Duke of Cambridge at Aldershot in 1871 and were finally laid up in 1947. The Drum Major positioned centrally behind the Colours is William Clark and from his medals it is possible to date the photograph to around 1888 since he received his Long Service & Good Conduct Medal in 1887 and was discharged after twenty-one years service in 1889.

The signallers of the 1st Battalion are shown with the equipment with which they communicated: flags, telescopes, heliographs and signalling lamps. Seated are Sergeant Vair, Lieutenant George Galbraith and Sergeant Anderson. Notice the specialist badge of crossed flags worn on the forearms.

The number of men employed in the Battalion Tailor's Shop is perhaps surprising but at this period sewing machines were in their infancy. The fitting and repair of doublets, jackets, trews and spats required considerable attention while kilt making was an additional skill to be mastered by regimental tailors.

The Battalion Provost Staff easily identified not only by the prominent 'MP' on their right wrists but also by the handcuffs and cell keys held by the two flanking men. Selected from amongst the toughest and smartest soldiers, their medals show that, with one exception, they are all veterans of the Egyptian campaigns.

While the 1st Battalion were on overseas service, the 2nd Battalion remained in home stations. One of its tasks was to provide reinforcements to the overseas battalion, particularly when it was on active service. No fewer than 1,000 men were posted to the 1st Battalion from the 2nd during the period of the operations in Egypt and the Sudan. Here the 2nd Battalion is seen marching at ease with weapons carried at personal preference through the countryside.

The 2nd Battalion remained in the South of England until 1885 when it was posted to the Curragh in Ireland with a detachment in Belfast, a city the Regiment would get to know better a century later. This photograph was taken in Aldershot the year before the move and shows the bearded Pipe Major George Stark, Piper Sharp and Colour Sergeant Walker standing. The seated figure with the dog on his lap is Captain George Silver and the figure in front is Piper McLeod.

In 1894 the 2nd Battalion moved to Edinburgh. Here the Battalion is drawn up on the Castle Esplanade with the Commanding Officer mounted on the right. He is Andrew Gilbert Wauchope who was to be killed a few years later while commanding the Highland Brigade during the Boer War at the Battle of Magersfontein. The subalterns marching the Colours onto parade are his cousin, Arthur Grenfell Wauchope, and 2nd Lieutenant Nicholas Edmonds who were wounded and killed at Magersfontein respectively. Major Alexander Duff, the Second in Command mounted in the centre was also wounded in the same battle but went on to command the 1st Battalion between 1902 and 1906. The officer in trews behind him is Quartermaster William Webb.

While the tradition of Highland dancing has always been maintained in the Regiment, the Pipes and Drums have invariably been its particular exponents. These four pipers are posing under the steady gaze of the Pipe Major William Bain. He was the son of Donald Bain who had been lauded for his piping during the battle as the 'Hero of the Alma'. William enlisted in 1880 and was with the 1st Battalion through the Egyptian campaigns, Malta and Gibraltar where he composed the tune 'The 42nd Farewell to Gibraltar'. His service continued as an instructor with a Volunteer Battalion and he deployed with some of them to the Boer War. He was still an instructor with the 6th Battalion during the early part of the First World War.

The establishment of the 2nd Battalion Officers Mess Staff seen here in Aldershot in 1884 grouped around the Mess Sergeant, Clark, seated to the right, and the bearded civilian chef, Mr Freshner. The two waiters holding silver salvers are Corporal Ross and Private Roberts. The silverman on the right is holding one of a pair of silver goblets of especial interest. Unbeknown to the Regiment, they were saved from the wreck of the troopship *Birkenhead* on which a detachment of the 73rd was sailing when it sank in 1852. One of the women who escaped in a lifeboat took them with her. It was only by chance that they were later discovered when put up for sale.

The 1st Perthshire Rifle Volunteers were raised in 1860 and are seen here in the early 1880s before they adopted Black Watch uniform in 1883. The tunics and trousers were coloured dark grey with scarlet facings and piping, the shakos dark blue. Seated second from the left is the Quartermaster, Captain John Simpson. He was one of four men of the 42nd to be awarded the Victoria Cross for bravery during the attack on Fort Rooyah on 15 April 1858. Then a Quartermaster Sergeant, he twice volunteered to go forward close to the parapet of the Fort under heavy fire and brought in an officer and a soldier who had been seriously wounded.

Three
From 1899 to 1913

The period between 1899 and 1913 is dominated by the South African or Boer War in which both battalions were to be involved. However, it was the 2nd Battalion which was first and most heavily committed. In all, the Regiment suffered the loss of fourteen officers and 194 other ranks during the war. Their names are commemorated on this magnificent memorial at the top of the Mound in Edinburgh. It was dedicated on 27 June 1910. The statue is the work of W. Birnie Rhynd.

On the outbreak of the Boer War, the 2nd Battalion was rapidly despatched to South Africa arriving in Cape Town in November 1899. It then moved to Modder River to join the Highland Brigade under Major General Andrew Wauchope who had previously commanded the Battalion. The Brigade formed part of the column tasked with the relief of Kimberley. Here members of the Battalion wait to move forward.

On the night of 10-11 December 1899 the Highland Brigade was ordered to carry out a dawn attack on positions the Boers had taken up to contest the advance to Kimberley. Unfortunately, this plan was not based on sufficient reconnaissance, the Boer positions were not located and the night march was delayed by thick undergrowth. The 2nd Battalion in the lead was caught in the open at first light in front of the Boer trenches. Pinned down, unable to move all day, the Battalion suffered 301 casualties. This simple memorial shows where the forty officers and men who died were buried. It has been replaced by a fine Celtic monument.

The 2nd Battalion went on to fight at Koodoesberg and Paardeberg in February 1900 and in other smaller actions. On each occasion there were further casualties. Here three officers are seen convalescing from their wounds. On the left, wounded at Magersfontein, is Second Lieutenant M. Drummond (later The Hon Sir Maurice Drummond). He was to be wounded again during the First World War after which he worked with the Metropolitan Police rising to Deputy Commissioner. Major The Hon Henry Maxwell in the centre was wounded at Paardeberg. He commanded the 2nd Battalion in 1903. The third officer is Christian Malise Hore-Ruthven.

This photograph not only demonstrates the living conditions under which the 2nd Battalion campaigned on the veldt in late 1899 and 1900, but also the type of terrain over which it operated. It is of a detachment camp and its primitive cookhouse.

The dress worn by the Regiment during the Boer War is well illustrated in this picture of Sergeant Johnstone and his section at Wilgo Bridge. This was the first campaign during which kilt aprons were worn but without the pouch in place of a sporran. The two types of headgear worn are the standard general service pith helmet and the slouch hat.

As the Boers were a particularly elusive enemy operating over a huge area, mobility played a vital part in the campaign. The Battalion transport consisted of a variety of local wagons pulled by a mixture of horses and mules.

After the surrender of Boers at Paardeberg and then the capture of Pretoria in June 1901, operations took on a different pattern with the Battalion marching in convoys over large distances after an ever-fleeting enemy. It was an enemy who would snipe at the troops from a distance and then scurry away on ponies. The lack of a sizeable cavalry and mounted infantry force was keenly felt.

This photograph and the one above it show the problems of crossing rivers on the march – although the jocks are experiencing little problem in wading barefoot through the shallows. The rivers were an important source of water in the wide, dry landscape of the veldt.

In the next stage of the war, the countryside was cordoned off into smaller areas in an attempt to counter the Boer advantage of mobility. This was only partially successful until barbed wire and block houses were substituted for troops. Here a wiring party from the Battalion is seen erecting a fence.

The other aspect of this new policy of cordoning in the Boers rather than chasing after their commandos, was the construction of block houses from which small sections of troops could dominate the barbed wire fences. In this photograph the roof is being positioned onto a block house which members of the Battalion have just constructed. Only one of the figures. is kilted as trousers are being worn for fatigues of this nature.

The 1st Battalion was despatched to South Africa from India in December 1901. There was an historic meeting of both battalions early the following year in Harrismith. By the very nature of the two battalion system, with one at home and one abroad, the chances of meeting were remote. There was to be only one other passing encounter in 1915 when the 2nd Battalion, leaving the line in France for Mesopotamia, marched through a village occupied by the 1st Battalion. The sergeants of both battalions are grouped together for a photograph in Harrismith.

On the same occasion as the picture above the officers of both the 1st and 2nd Battalions pose for a photograph in Harrismith. The commanding officers were respectively Edward Grogan, who had been wounded in the Ashanti Campaign, and Carthew-Yorstoun, who had been wounded at Magersfontein. While in Harrismith, the 1st Battalion created a large '42' on the hillside which remains to this day and its name given to the adjacent '42nd Township'.

The 1st Battalion moved to Fort George in 1904. The central figure of this group is sounding the gong captured by the 42nd at Serai Ghat in 1857 during the Indian Mutiny. Ever since, it has accompanied the Battalion and being positioned near the Guardroom has been – and still is – used to sound the hours. On the left is Company Sergeant Major William Fowler who had joined the Regiment twenty years previously. In 1911 he was commissioned as Quartermaster of the 1st Battalion which appointment he retained for the duration of the First World War. He served on until 1931 when he became Curator of the Regimental Museum.

A rare photograph of the Officers' Mess laid out for a party with much of the silver displayed in the bow window. Prominent and largest amongst these pieces is the Highland Society of London Vase presented to the 42nd as a 'mark of esteem and appreciation' of the Regiment's part in the battle of Alexandria in 1801. On the table in front of it the silver mounted ram's head snuff mull is alleged to have been used as an ink stand during the Crimean War.

At the end of the Boer War, the 2nd Battalion proceeded to India. This photograph was taken in 1906 or 1907 and shows the Battalion threading its way along after attending Church Parade in the Garrison Chapel in Cherat.

The Machine Gun Section of the 2nd Battalion with their weapons and mules whilst in Peshawar in 1907. Seven miles away in the distance is the entry to the Khyber Pass. The left hand gun is manned by Sergeant Lambert, the other by Sergeant Hannan. The officer in the centre is Lieutenant A.P. Wavell (later Field Marshal Earl Wavell of Cyrenaica and Winchester).

In December 1911 the 2nd Battalion received the distinction of furnishing the Guard of Honour on the steps of the throne at the Coronation Durbar in Delhi. The King Emperor told the Commanding Officer, Lieutenant Colonel William Campbell that the 'Regiment looked magnificent – as they always do. The Guard of Honour was quite wonderful'. He then ordered an additional grant of Delhi Durbar Medals for every man in the Guard. The following year HM King George V was to become Colonel-in-Chief of the Regiment.

In the final years of peace before the outbreak of the First World War, officers of the 2nd Battalion are photographed in 1812 period costume of the 42nd at the Centenary Ball in Government House, Calcutta, December 1912. Seven of the fifteen officers in the picture were to lose their lives in action within four years. Amongst these was The Hon Fergus Bowes-Lyon (standing fifth from the right) who died at Loos in September 1915. He was a brother of HM Queen Elizabeth, The Queen Mother.

Four
From 1914 to 1918

Just as the sheer scale of the First World War was unlike that of any previous conflict, so too was The Black Watch's involvement in it on a different scale to any of its former engagements. Fourteen front-line battalions of the Regiment fought in the war principally, but not entirely, in France and Belgium. There the conflict soon stabilized into a trench warfare which was to last four years. These men of the 6th (Perthshire) Battalion are members of the staff of the Officers' Mess and seem to have acquired a bottle of wine for themselves. Notice the style of bonnet without a toorie which was on issue during much of the war.

Another photograph showing men of the Regiment in a fairly typical trench on a fine day. Even then, however, there was the perpetual danger from snipers, from mortars and artillery harassing fire.

The initial shock of the German invasion of Belgium in 1914 was met by the regular troops of the British Expeditionary Force which included the 1st Battalion then stationed in Aldershot. Thereupon, the Territorial Army was mobilized and expanded while later on further battalions were raised as part of Kitchener's 'New Army'. Here recruits of the 3/5th Battalion from Angus are seen in their mess tent set up in the South School, Forfar, in July 1915.

The first action of the 4th Battalion was in the heavy fighting at the Battle of Neuve Chapelle in March 1915 in which the 2nd and 5th Battalions also played a part. The photograph of the village was taken just after it had been captured. Despite a bombardment of the German position by 500 British guns prior to the assault, the crucifix remains unscathed. The officer below it is 2nd Lieutenant W.C.O. Barrie. He was twice wounded before being killed the following year.

This rather indistinct photograph appeared in a newspaper shortly after the Battle of Neuve Chapelle and shows members of D Company of the 4th Battalion on their objective with their company commander, Captain Leslie Boase, standing in the trench coat on the right. He was wounded at the Battle of Aubers Ridge two months later and was to lose his life in the attack on High Wood on the Somme in July 1916 whilst serving with the 7th Battalion.

Despite the conditions of life in the trenches, it was still possible to maintain standards of turnout as demonstrated by Regimental Sergeant Major J.C. 'Punch' Wilson of the 6th Battalion seen in front of his dugout at Fauquissart in July 1915. He spent the entire war with the Battalion becoming Quartermaster in 1916, was three times mentioned in despatches and awarded the Military Cross.

The venerable commanding officer of the 6th Battalion in his reinforced dugout 'Castle Stalker', Campbell Avenue, in Authuille. Sir Robert Moncrieffe, Bart, joined the Perthshire Militia in 1874 and, after regular service, joined the 1st Perthshire Volunteer Battalion in 1884. This unit later became the 6th Battalion. He commanded it for eighteen years up until 1911, but rejoined on the outbreak of war, at the age of fifty-nine.

The mud and cold of the trenches during the winter could be horrendous but the clothing to combat it had improved by 1915-1916. This officer is wearing the sheepskin jerkin and the trousers provided for the troops. He is Lieutenant N.F. Dixon who later served with the Machine Gun Corps and was to be killed in action in October 1917.

Even in more temperate weather the conditions in the trenches were extremely unpleasant as well as dangerous. Here jocks of the Auchterarder Company are seen picking lice out of their clothing.

There were very few comforts available during active service on the Western Front, but one of these was the rum ration issued after an action or hard spell of trench work. Here men of the 8th Battalion queue to receive their tot after the Battle of Longueval in July 1916. This was the first of the New Army battalions raised by the Regiment.

The Pipes and Drums playing after the 8th Battalion had captured Longueval on the Somme. This was during a lull in the fighting for the Germans counter attacked with vigour and the position changed hands several times over a period of five days during which twenty-five officers and 470 other ranks of the Battalion became casualties.

While in the trenches constant watch had to be kept for any signs of enemy activity. However, exposure above the trench parapet involved great danger from sniper fire. The solution was found in the use of simple periscopes.

With the introduction by the Germans of chemical warfare into the conflict, troops had to improvise protection and then wear ever more sophisticated respirators. The first gasses used were vapour only, but with the later use of liquid chemicals, notably mustard gas, troops had to protect all exposed skin, making the kilt a much less viable garment.

While there were inevitably periods of intense activity when attacks were carried out or enemy assaults had to be countered, there were also long periods of static defence of trench lines. In addition, there had to be much work maintaining and expanding the trench system and repairing damage caused by artillery fire. Here a working party poses for a photograph during a break.

Just as the routine of maintenance to trenches had to be carried out, so too did the routine of life have to continue at the front and amongst these the repair of clothing. Corporal Irvine is seen in his makeshift tailor's shop at Bray during the summer of 1916.

By far the most potent battalion weapon was the machine gun which could have a devastating effect on assaulting enemy infantry. Here one is seen in the trenches near La Boisselle which the 6th Battalion took over from the French in August 1915 and continued to occupy for the next five months. On the left is Sergeant McCartney with Major Calder and Captain Dixon.

This group of men on the left have just come out of the line which accounts for their cheerful expressions. They are collecting their packs before moving back to a rest area.

Whenever possible simple graves were dug for members of the Regiment who died on active service. This British Cemetery at Locon contained those of the 6th Battalion who were killed whilst holding that sector of the line in mid-June 1915. The second grave from the left is that of Lieutenant R.P. Haldane, the first of fifty-five officers of the Battalion to be killed during the war.

The 10th Battalion spent less than two months on the Western Front before it was moved to Salomika in November 1915 to face the possible invasion there by the Bulgarians. After experiencing bitter winter weather with insufficient equipment the Battalion is seen here marching to Ambarkoi in the searing heat of June 1916. It was then involved in some desultory trench warfare before returning to France two years later in the middle of 1918.

On the outbreak of war, the 2nd Battalion was in India but was soon moved to France and took part in the battles of Neuve Chapelle, Festubert and Loos – amongst others. Then, in December 1915 it was despatched as a reinforcement to the Mesopotamia Expedition. There, after incurring heavy losses fighting the Turks, the Battalion was the first unit to enter Bagdad when it was captured in March 1917. It was here from Samarra railway station shown in the photograph that it took the trophy, the Bagdad Bell, which was to remain with the Battalion for the remainder of its existence.

Throughout most of the war, the 3rd Battalion was involved in training reinforcements for the other battalions of the Regiment at Nigg on the Cromarty Firth, but in November 1917 it was moved to Ireland. The squad in this photograph may look a little incongruous in their pith helmets at Nigg in May 1916 but are a draft destined for the 2nd Battalion in Mesopotamia.

After the collapse of Turkish resistance in Mesopotamia the 2nd Battalion joined General Allenby's forces in Palestine in time to take part in his brilliant victory at Megiddo on 19 September 1918. Taken around midday, this photograph shows the troops on the objective at Khez Zerkiyeh having had only two men killed and accounting for around a thousand Turkish prisoners. The Adjutant is standing in the centre. He is Captain Ritchie and was awarded the Military Cross for his part in the battle (later General Sir Neil Ritchie, he was appointed Colonel of The Regiment in 1950). Seated in front is the Medical Officer, Captain Moore Cameron and, on the right, Captain W.D. McEwan MC, commanding No.1 Company.

As a fitting conclusion to the Regiment's part in the First World War, this group is the 1st Battalion triumphant on German soil at Roisdorf which it reached on 23 December 1918. But victory had been won at an appalling cost: the Regiment lost around 8,000 men killed and over 20,000 wounded during the four years of the conflict.

Five

From 1919 to 1939

The interwar years saw the return to the system of regiments generally having one battalion stationed abroad while the other was based at home. It was the turn of the 1st Battalion to spend most of this period in India. This dramatic photograph shows the Hill Detachment on parade at Lebong in the foothills of the Himalayas.

After the war, the 2nd Battalion formed part of the Army of Occupation on the Rhine based near Cologne. In March 1921 it was sent to Lublinitz in Upper Silesia to help oversee the plebiscite which was to decide whether that should become German or Polish territory. In order to ensure strict impartiality, no fraternization was permitted with the local population but this did not inhibit harmony with the French and Italian contingents seen in this group of allied soldiers.

During the eighteen consecutive years which the 1st Battalion spent in India from 1919, it moved station five times, the first being to Quetta. This route march shows the Military Band with their percussionists in front of the wind instruments, an unusual arrangement.

The number of recruits requiring training during the First World War had far exceeded the capacity of the Depot in Perth and was carried out elsewhere. After the war, Queen's Barracks returned to its former role. Here, at the entrance to the Barracks members of the staff pay their respects to their comrades who fell at the Battle of Loos in 1915, a battle in which six battalions of the Regiment fought simultaneously taking very heavy casualties.

In May 1921 the Crown Prince Hirohito of Japan arrived in Perth by train on his way to stay with the Duke and Duchess of Atholl. A Guard of Honour of Reservists was mounted in Station Square commanded by Major Charles Henderson. These were all veterans of the First World War and no fewer than eight of those on parade had been awarded the Distinguished Conduct Medal and sixteen the Military Medal. Two decades later, members of the Regiment would be fighting Hirohito's forces in Burma.

In 1926 the 2nd Battalion was stationed in Fort George. This group shows those members of the Battalion who had previously served there with the 1st Battalion in 1906. On the left is Major Francis Chalmer. He was later to command the Battalion in 1933. The others are Company Sergeant Major W. Reid, Regimental Quartermaster Sergeant G. Morrison, Sergeant J. Watson, Regimental Sergeant Major A. Mathison, Colour Sergeant D. Stevenson, Lance Sergeant G. Mcintosh, Sergeant J. Robertson and Private W. Ramsley. In the background hangs the 'Bagdad Bell' captured by the Battalion in 1916.

Whenever possible, Highland Games have been a central fixture in the Regiment's annual diary. This group of Senior non commissioned officers was taken at the 2nd Battalion Games in May 1932 in Colchester where it had moved to after Fort George. They are Sergeant D. Macintosh, Sergeant J. Cowan, In-Pensioner C. Harrower, Sergeant D. Mackenzie and Sergeant G. Wilkinson. Harrower had enlisted in the Regiment fifty-seven years before, in 1875, and is wearing the Egyptian Medal and Khedive's Star.

While in India, the 1st Battalion undertook periodic 'flag marches' to ensure that the British military presence was seen by the general public. Here members of the Battalion have a break in one such march, those in the foreground being part of the Military Band.

At much the same time that the 1st Battalion were pictured taking a break on a march in the top photograph this cheerful group of jocks from the 2nd Battalion were also enjoying a break while on a march. At this time the Battalion was based in Glasgow but carried out its 1935 field training in the Regiment's recruiting area.

The Indian Platoon was responsible for looking after the mules which carried the Vickers Machine Guns. Members of these platoons did not move with battalions between stations so these individuals were only with the 1st Battalion while it was in Barrackpore between 1934 and 1936. Those of the Regiment seated in front are Lieutenant George Campbell Preston (who commanded the 1st Battalion in 1951), 'Bud' Howie (who was to be commissioned in the field in 1940 but taken prisoner of war shortly afterwards at St Valery), Captain William Bucknall, Captain William Dundas, Lieutenant C.M.G. Blair (who was to command the 1st Battalion briefly in 1943 before being severely wounded in Sicily later that year) and Company Quartermaster Sergeant Monzie.

In 1934 the 2nd Battalion provided the central feature of that year's Royal Tournament in Olympia when over 400 men appeared in a regimental pageant. This included one company seen here in period costume of 1745 in which they demonstrated the drill movements at the time of the Regiment's first battle, Fontenoy. It is interesting to note that the Royal Tournament was the brainchild of a Black Watch Officer, Colonel Sir Malcolm Fox who was largely responsible for its inauguration in 1900.

His Majesty King George V was Colonel in Chief of the Regiment from 3 September 1912. A year before his death he inspected the Guard formed by the 2nd Battalion when he arrived at Ballater Station on his way to Balmoral on 21 August 1935. The Guard Commander is Major Charles Gilmour. Wounded in the First World War, he went on to command the 16th Battalion, The Royal Fusiliers, during the Second World War.

After the First World War the 4th and 5th Battalions were amalgamated into 4/5th Battalion. New colours were presented to this battalion on 10 August 1935 by the then Duchess of York at Glamis Castle, her childhood home. This was nearly two years before she became Colonel-in-Chief of the Regiment. She is seen here holding Princess Margaret by the hand and accompanied by the HRH The Duke of York (later King George VI) in the uniform of the Queen's Own Cameron Highlanders. Behind, bringing the cased colours from the Castle are Company Quartermaster Sergeant J. Forbes, the Colonel of the Regiment, Lieutenant General Sir Archibald R. Cameron and Company Sergeant Major J. Maguire.

The end of an era came when the horse passed out of service as a transport animal in the Regiment. Mules would be used in various theatres by battalions during the Second World War and later. This photograph is the last picture of the 2nd Battalion Horsed Transport and it was taken in April 1937 in Maryhill Barracks, Glasgow, before leaving on overseas service.

During the latter part of 1937, both regular battalions were overseas. The 1st Battalion spent the year in Khartoum on its way homeward from India, while the 2nd Battalion was sent as a reinforcement to the British Forces in Palestine and Trans-Jordan to help prevent conflict between the Jews and Arabs. Here 'A' Company stands by watching a Jewish demonstration in Jerusalem.

The duties carried out in Palestine in aid of the civil power were wide-ranging from riot control to cordon and search, picquets, escort and ambushes, some in the urban areas around Jerusalem, others in the mountainous northern areas. Those wearing tam o'shanters (TOS) on and next to the truck in this photograph are members of the Mortar Platoon. Platoon Sergeant Major Elder is seated on the left with Private Fraser and Lance Corporal Dickson. Standing are Private McLaren, Humphries, Turnball, Hird and Watson.

The number of orders of dress has always been large in a Highland regiment with variations for kilt and trews but this was compounded in a country like Palestine where there were different weather conditions in summer and winter. This photograph shows men of the 2nd Battalion arranged in a sample of them. After the stick orderly on the left come three in Emergency Order, Summer, then members of the Pipes and Drums in Full Dress, both Summer and Winter. The remainder are in pairs in Drill Order, Summer, Winter Dry Weather, Winter Trews, Winter Wet Weather.

As war with Nazi Germany became ever more likely, the Territorial battalions of the Regiment expanded and prepared themselves for active service once more. Men of the 6/7th Battalion from Perthshire and Fife are seen rehearsing their drills for combating low-flying aircraft.

With the imminence of war training at the Depot took on a new urgency. This recruit squad passed out at the time of the Munich Crisis. The Squad Sergeant is T. Fell and the officer Major W.R. Bucknall, who had been attached to the Royal Flying Corps during the First World War and been shot down in flames from 6,000 feet. He would go on to command the 1st Battalion The Worcestershire Regiment during the Second World War. Seated next to Piper A. Morrison on the right is Private Bill Lark, also a piper himself. He was to see action in Crete, the Western Desert and as a muleteer with the 2nd Battalion in Burma in 1944. There a set of pipes was to be dropped to him by parachute. Behind him is Private James Clarkin who was taken prisoner of war in 1940 and was murdered by SS guards while being marched between prison camps on 24 April 1945 just weeks before the end of the conflict.

Six
From 1939 to 1945

During the Second World War, battalions of the Regiment were in action in almost every theatre of the war, from France in 1940 to Somaliland, North Africa, Crete, Syria, Sicily, Italy, as 'Chindits' in Burma and on to the final route to victory across North-West Europe. This photograph shows Pipe Major Rab Roy 'the piper of Tobruk'. Although he was wounded more than once himself, he was still playing for some of the less serious casualties in the Regimental Aid Post after the attempted breakout from that besieged fortress by the 2nd Battalion. The Pipe Major had previously been made prisoner of war in Crete but managed to escape after being made to play at a German officers dinner in Athens.

'Has everyone got a Brush, Shoe, Small?' Even before the declaration of war conscription was introduced and here men from the Regimental area are being kitted out on arrival in Queens Barracks in July 1939. On the right is the Quartermaster, Captain (later Major) Peter Hitchman. He was of the generation which saw action in both world wars, enlisting in 1908 and retiring in 1946.

After the outbreak of war three battalions of the Regiment were despatched to France and Belgium and took part in the retreat to the Channel ports in face of the German 'Blitzkreig' in May 1940. After much stiff fighting, the 1st Battalion was finally forced to surrender with most of the 51st Highland Division at St Valery, while the 4th Battalion managed to escape through Le Havre. The 6th Battalion was in a different division and was evacuated at Dunkirk. It was then deployed in defence of the Isle of Wight. The lamentable lack of appropriate equipment is evident in this picture of the Anti-Tank Platoon on patrol on the island lead by Lieutenant (later Major) H.C.B. McDuff-Duncan who would later be wounded in North Africa.

As a separate regiment, the Tyneside Scottish had six battalions in the First World War. In 1939 the 1st Battalion The Tyneside Scottish was revived and became a battalion of The Black Watch until 1944, when the 70th Infantry Brigade was broken up. The remaining officers and men were split up as reinforcements to other Scottish battalions. Before then it had put up some heroic actions in France in 1940, had lost many men as prisoners of war but had been re-formed and sent to Iceland. During its year there it had only one man killed who was hit by a stray bullet when a lone German Heinkel aircraft attacked in February 1941. This photograph shows Private Martin Hunter's funeral.

For obvious reasons there is little photographic record of the lives of those of the 1st Battalion taken captive at St Valery during the five years they were held in Germany and Poland. This picture of amateur dramatics shows how they did their best to pass the time. Some of the jocks worked on farms or in the mines, some few managed to escape – particularly in the early stages – but there can be no denying that this was a most terrible fate for professional soldiers during a war.

As the 2nd Battalion were in Palestine on the outbreak of war, it was thrown into a very different type of conflict from those battalions deployed to oppose the Germans in France and Belgium. Their first fight was against the Italians in Somaliland but the collapse of French resistance in their part of the country left the Battalion outnumbered and outflanked. After a successful withdrawal, the Battalion was next in action in Crete. While defending the important airfield at Heraklion it was subjected to the very first parachute assault, preceded by the heavy air bombardment seen in the photograph. The Battalion held its ground resolutely. In the words of the Commander of the German parachute battalion: 'The battle continued with great ferocity for two days. The Black Watch never surrendered. Had it been any other regiment, any other, all would have been well. Eventually, we were at our wit's end.'

After evacuation from Crete the 2nd Battalion found itself in Syria facing the Vichy French. Fortunately, an armistice was signed before the Battalion was required to assault their almost impregnable position in the Jebel. On the right of the picture as the column winds up into the hills is Lieutenant Bill Swannell, who was later to win the Military Cross.

The next assignment given to the 2nd Battalion in their enormously varied war was to join the besieged garrison of Tobruk. There, on 20 November 1941, the Battalion was to take part in a breakout with armoured support to coincide with an advance by the 8th Army. Unfortunately, the tanks set off at a tangent and The Black Watch attack went in unsupported. In the face of terrible German machine gun and artillery fire, the objective was reached but by all too few of those who had crossed the start line an hour before. Here, remnants of 13 Platoon occupy positions they captured – in the near trench are 2nd Lieutenant Macdonald and Corporal Wallace.

The Commanding Officer, Lieutenant Colonel George Rusk speaking to survivors of the breakout from Tobruk, an action in which the 2nd Battalion lost twenty-five officers and over 300 men either killed or wounded, the Commanding Officer being amongst the wounded. 'Ruskie', as he was normally termed, had won his Miliary Cross during the First World War and brought the experience gained during that conflict to lead the Battalion with great skill and flair in this action. Years later he was to oversee the setting up of the Regimental Museum in Balhousie Castle.

In June 1942, two years after the surrender at St Valery, the re-formed 51st Highland Division, fully trained and equipped, arrived in Egypt in time to take a major role in the Battle of El Alamein. There were three battalions of the Regiment in the Division: the resurrected 1st Battalion, the 5th and the 7th Battalions. Men from the last of these, the Fife Territorial Battalion are pictured marching across the arid North African desert.

Shortly before El Alamein, intensive preparatory training was carried out in the desert. During that period, this photograph was taken of a group from the 7th Battalion. They are the Medical Officer Dr McGowan, Captain Sandy Scott, who was later to be wounded and taken prisoner, Lieutenant (later Captain) Douglas Selbie, Captain Norman Millar (standing), who was to be wounded at El Alamein, and the driver of the carrier, Private Melville.

All three Black Watch battalions in the 51st Highland Division took part in the Battle of El Alamein in October 1942 and each captured its objective successfully. After the battle, the 8th Army followed close on the retreating enemy. Initially there was little resistance, the main delay being caused by mines and demolitions. Here a squad from the 7th Battalion under Captain Simon Ramsay (later Earl of Dalhousie, KT) labour to prepare a by-pass around a blown bridge near the ancient Roman city of Leptis Magna. Captain Ramsay was taken prisoner later in the North African campaign but managed to escape while being held in Italy.

Men of B Company of the 5th Battalion listen intently to the briefing by their Company Commander, Major (later Colonel) John McGregor at Gabes in Tunisia, April 1943. It was near here that the Germans were to contest hotly defensive positions at Mareth and Wadi Akarit.

Using a jerry can as a table, intent on his task, Piper McLaren composes a pipe tune to commemorate the Battle of El Alamein in an olive grove near Gabes some six months after the event.

Often referred to as the 'Highway Decorators' members of the 51st Highland Division were immensely proud of their reputation and of their Divisional sign which they portrayed at every opportunity. This picture was taken in Sfax which was reached on 10 April 1943. These two have been identified as Privates James Bruce and Alec McMichael.

Having fought their way across Libya, members of the Regiment were astonished by the reception they received on entering Sfax, the first town reached in Tunisia. There they were heralded as 'liberators'. Hastily pipers were drawn in from the companies and a 5th Battalion Pipe Band formed. The Pipe Major on the left is Alec Herd and beside him Ronnie Simpson and then Ian Simpson. The Drum Major is probably Jim Massie and the Bass Drummer co-opted for the occasion but not visible in the photograph was the Padre, the Reverend Tom Nicoll.

While the 1st, 5th and 7th Battalions were fighting their way west from Egypt, through Libya and into Tunisia, the 6th Battalion entered the conflict from Algeria in March 1943 as part of the 1st Army and came into Tunisia from the other side, fighting a notable action at Sidi Medienne. Thereafter the 6th spent the remainder of the war in the Italian Campaign taking part in the momentous battles to break the Gothic Line. Here a 6-pounder anti-tank detachment relaxes near Monte Cassino in May 1944. They are Frank Bailey, a despatch rider who was to be wounded shortly afterwards, Lance Corporal Nicol, wearing the steel helmet, and Sergeant Charlie Wynd, reading.

The 2nd Battalion had already opposed the Italians in Somaliland, the French in Syria and the Germans in Crete and at Tobruk. Next it was sent to India to face the Japanese advance through Burma. Then in late 1943, it was specially trained as two 'Chindit Columns' to operate behind Japanese lines as part of General Ord Wingate's force. The photograph shows men of the Battalion carrying out the arduous preparatory training.

In March 1944 the two Black Watch Chindit columns (suitably numbered 42 and 73) were airlifted by Dakotas to a base in the Burmese jungle. From there they began their operations against the Japanese, patrolling, laying ambushes and carrying out demolitions. This was to last for five months under the most appalling conditions of heat, monsoon rains and disease. Here a mule is resisting being loaded aboard one of the aircraft in India before the Battalion deployed.

The whole concept of the Chindit operations depended upon resupply by air. This generally worked well in the earlier stages. Nevertheless, each man was carrying a weight of some 70lbs and the animal transport played a crucial role in providing the necessary mobility to maintain surprise and avoid being caught by the Japanese. Here men and mules are trained in crossing water obstacles of which there were many in Northern Burma.

Eventually the remnants of the 2nd Battalion marched out of the jungle after their ordeal during the Chindit Campaign, worn down by fatigue and sickness. Only two officers and forty-eight men were passed fit to continue. Yet the astonishing variety of tasks undertaken by the Battalion during the war was not yet over. After being nursed back to health, the Battalion was converted to the parachute role. This group are seen prepared for their first practice jump with Lieutenant Colonel Douglas Ross in the centre.

Unlike the 2nd Battalion which had such a diversity of roles, the 4th Battalion missed most of the action during the war. After evacuation from France in 1940, it was sent to defend Gibraltar against anticipated attack through Fascist Spain. This never materialized but the Battalion spent nearly three years on the 'Rock' during which time it improved the defences enormously, tunnelling copiously.

From North Africa the 51st Highland Division took part in the invasion of Sicily but was then withdrawn to Britain in preparation for the invasion of North West Europe. The 5th Battalion landed in Normandy on 'D' Day, 6 June 1944, to be followed a few days later by the 1st and 7th Battalions – as did the 1st Battalion, The Tyneside Scottish, in 49th Division. After a bloody defence of the Chateau of Breville, the 5th Battalion moved on. This mortar team are seen in action near Herouvillette midway between there and Colombelles, their next major action. All three battalions were then involved in the breakout from Caen and the battles around the Falaise salient.

In September 1944 the 51st Highland Division returned to St Valery where the original Division had been forced to surrender in June 1940. The Divisional Commander is seen here with Monsieur Le Maire and Monsieur Le Curé of St Valery. Major General Tom Rennie joined the Regiment in 1919, had been with the Division at the time of the surrender at St Valery but had managed to escape. He commanded the 5th Battalion in North Africa. Sadly, he was to be killed in action as the Division was crossing the Rhine in March 1945.

After the breakout from Normandy, the advance through France and Belgium was rapid. Everywhere the jocks were received with delight by those they were liberating but none more so than the pipers. Here in Le Deliverande, Piper J. McNally from Lochee, Dundee, and Piper J. Yardley of Kirkcaldy are welcomed by some of the local inhabitants.

Once in Holland, the German resistance stiffened and, during the winter of 1944-1945 the 1st, 5th and 7th Battalions were all involved in a series of actions leading up to the Battle of the Reichswald Forest. However, before then, in January 1945, they had been rushed south to face the last German offensive in the Ardennes in intense cold. Then it was back to the Reichswald and the capture of the towns of Gennep and Goch. This rare action shot shows a section crossing a street dominated by spandau machine gun fire under cover of a smoke grenade.

Now well into Germany, the 51st Highland Division reached Goch, the last town before the Rhine and part of the Siegfried Line. Members of the 5th Battalion are seen entering the north of the town on 18 February 1945. Their initial objective was taken with reasonable ease but they were later required to assist against the stiffer resistance to the south of the town.

On the night of 23 of March 1945 men of the three Black Watch battalions in the 51st Highland Division were ferried across the Rhine under cover of artillery barrage and a massive smoke screen. They are seen here moving forward in 'Kangaroos'. The HD 69 signifies the 7th Battalion. Little opposition was met before they were established on the far bank. The credit for being the first British troops across the Rhine fell to this battalion.

German resistance did not ease once the Rhine had been crossed. There was stiff fighting in Rees on 24 March where men of the 5th Battalion are seen in house-to-house fighting through the streets of the town. Such was the esteem in which he was held, that news of the death of the Divisional Commander, Major General Tom Rennie, during the Crossing of the Rhine, was deliberately kept from the troops until the action was over. He was temporarily replaced by the Commander of 154 Highland Brigade, Brigadier James Oliver, who on the outbreak of war had been a Major in the 4/5th Battalion. He is believed to be the only Territorial officer ever to have commanded a division in action.

The two pictures on this page show the more human side of life for the jocks in the final stages of the war in north west Europe. In this one men of the 1st Battalion are cooking in a battered farmhouse in Germany.

Remembering it was Shrove Tuesday, Private 'Sunny' Barton borrowed some flour from somewhere and a frying pan. Still complete in fighting order, he set to making pancakes. He added the rag as an apron saying: 'I don't want to get messed up.'

April 1945 and the war virtually over, the battalions which had fought their way across France, Belgium and Holland were now into the heart of Northern Germany approaching Bremen. Sergeant Ross of the Anti-Tank Platoon of the 7th Battalion is pictured in front of a 17-pounder gun.

In the ruined streets of Bremerhaven the Victory Parade took place on 15 May 1945. Some of these soldiers of the Regiment, but only some few, had fought all the long hard route through North Africa, Sicily and across Northern Europe. Casualties had been heavy and consequent changes in personnel frequent. As an example it was estimated that the 5th Battalion alone had lost ninety-six officers and some 950 other ranks killed or wounded during this period.

Without doubt one of the most colourful characters of the Regiment and one of its bravest wartime officers was Major (later Lieutenant Colonel) Alec Brodie. Serving with the Polish forces in the earlier part of the war, it was not until Normandy in 1944 that he was to serve with the 5th Battalion. Between then and the end of the conflict, he was to be wounded three times and to be awarded a Military Cross for gallantry at Colombelles and a DSO at Goch. In typical style he is photographed joining the Battalion Games in Steyerburg during the summer of 1945 mounted with a makeshift band. Seated beside him is Captain Angus Stroyan.

After the long hard fight up the Italian mainland, the 6th Battalion was taken out of the line in December 1944 and despatched to Greece. There it was to assist in holding down the Communist (ELAS) insurgency at first in Athens and later in the hills near Mount Parnassus. In May 1946 the Battalion held its final parade in Greece before being demobilized. The Inspecting Officer is Major General A. Adair and the Commanding Officer is Lieutenant Colonel Brian Madden who had been wounded four times and commanded both the 6th Battalion and the 1st Battalion The Gordon Highlanders.

Seven
From 1946 to 1954

The two features which dominated this period for the Regiment were the retreat from Empire and the Cold War, including the conflict in Korea. In this photograph the entire 1st Battalion is shown marshalled on parade as part of the garrison of the Allied sectors of Berlin in 1951. The support weapons are on either flank, machine guns, mortars and anti-tank guns with the bands behind them and the reconnaissance and transport vehicles at the rear and edges. The Commanding Officer is Lieutenant Colonel G.P. Campbell-Preston.

While the 2nd Battalion was in Peshawar in 1905, it had carved a badge in the rock face at Cherat, a hill station which provided some relief from the summer heat. The Battalion was there again in 1947 during the period just before the partition of India. There it was involved in tasks connected with the referendum in the North West Frontier Province. Before leaving Cherat for the last time a subsidiary scroll '1947' was added. Standing alongside is Pipe Major John McNicol.

On 26 February 1948 the 2nd Battalion The Black Watch were the last British troops to leave Pakistan when they embarked at Karachi – the last of a very long line of regiments which had served in the sub-continent. Before leaving, it had given a Royal Salute to the Quaid-e-Azam, new head of state, Mohammed Ali Jinnah, and are pictured marching past him heading for the docks.

Only a month after leaving India the 2nd Battalion held its last parade before having to amalgamate with the 1st. That this reduction would be of only relatively short duration was not known at the time. This photograph of the Guardroom at Duisburg symbolizes the amalgamation. On the left is the 2nd Battalion's 'Bagdad Bell' and on the right the Indian Mutiny Gong of the 1st Battalion. In the centre is Sergeant J. Hocknull who had enlisted as a boy-soldier ten years previously in 1938.

At least four decades before it became the practice to have women attached to an infantry battalion, Major Kathleen ('Mick') Prendergast, an Australian, was posted as Medical Officer to the 1st Battalion in 1947. This may have been a leg-pull in the expectation that the Regiment would protest violently… but it didn't! Described by one of her commanding officers as 'caustic, forthright, skilful, quarrelsome, devoted, friendly and passionately pro-Black Watch', she soon wove her way into the very fabric of the Battalion. She served it for five years, an unusually long tour, and was granted permission by the Colonel of The Regiment, Lord Wavell, to wear the Red Hackle in her bonnet and a Black Watch tartan skirt – much to the dismay of the RAMC authorities. She is pictured with him at the athletics meeting in 1948.

The old Colours of the 1st Battalion are laid up in Perth in 1948. More correctly they are those of the 42nd for they were presented by HRH The Duke of Cambridge in 1871 before the 42nd and 73rd were amalgamated. They are believed to have been the last Colours carried in the British Army to bear the old regimental number. They are being received into safe keeping by Earl Wavell, the Colonel of The Regiment, and are now held in the Regimental Museum.

The Colonel of The Regiment, Field Marshal The Earl Wavell, died on 24 May 1950 and his funeral took place in Westminster Abbey. As a 19 gun salute was fired from the Tower of London, his flag-draped coffin was borne from it by non-commissioned officers of The Black Watch and set on board the launch for the journey upstream to Westminster. Later, they were to lower the coffin into his grave at Winchester College. Without question the greatest son of the Regiment, he was also a great champion of the Regimental system.

As Commander-in-Chief, North Atlantic Treaty Organization, General Dwight D. Eisenhower (later President of the United States of America) inspects the Guard of Honour formed by 'D' Company in Berlin in 1951. During the war, while on a secret visit to Gibraltar, he had been apprehended by a sentry of the 4th Battalion and held in the guardroom for a couple of hours before his true identity was revealed. The Guard Commander is Major J.B.F. Fortune whose father, Major General Sir Victor Fortune, commanded the 51st Highland Division at St Valery in 1940. The Colour Ensign is Second Lieutenant A.M. Gomme Duncan and the escorts Sergeants Bromich and Robertson.

Shortly before the 1st Battalion left for Korea in 1952, the Colonel-in-Chief journeyed to Crail to bid it godspeed in the action ahead of it. This was Her Majesty's first public engagement as Queen Mother, whilst the Court was still in mourning for HM King George VI. This gesture was much appreciated by all members of the Regiment. In this picture she is accompanied by the newly appointed Colonel of The Regiment, Major General Neil McMicking, who had commanded the 2nd Battalion in Palestine just before the war. Her Majesty is shaking hands with Captain (Quartermaster) Patrick Goudy. He had enlisted as a drummer boy at the age of fourteen in 1887.

The 1st Battalion landed in Korea on 21 June 1952. Three weeks later it was undertaking its first month in the line. While relatively quiet by comparison with the actions on the Hook in November the Battalion nevertheless lost two officers and ten private soldiers who died during this period. Checking details on the map with the Commanding Officer are Major Peter Buchanan, Major (later Sir Robert) Macrae of the Seaforth Highlanders and Major (later Brigadier) Pat Douglas, who was the only member of the 1st Battalion to have proceeded on active service with it in 1939 to France, in 1942 to North Africa, in 1944 to Normandy and in 1952 to Korea. The Commanding Officer is Lieutenant Colonel David Rose and, on the right, the Adjutant, Captain (later Colonel) Earle Nicoll.

The climate and the fighting were to become much harsher later in the year but these jocks of 11 Platoon, 'D' Company are evidently enjoying their lunch in the summer sunshine. They are Private Robertson, Lance Corporal Muirhead, Private Struman and Lance Corporal Findlay.

'C' Company command post with, on the right, the Company Commander Major (later Lieutenant Colonel) Malcolm Wallace of that Ilk, and Captain (later Colonel) The Hon David Arbuthnott. Both officers had fathers who served in the Regiment and in the latter's case was Colonel of The Regiment (Major General The Viscount of Arbuthnott). In turn both Malcolm Wallace and David Arbuthnott would become Regimental Secretaries.

A delegation of three United States generals visits the Battalion command post. On the left is Pipe Major Erickson who was to be seriously wounded during the action on the Hook, on the right is Lance Corporal McNie. The Commanding Officer, Lieutenant Colonel David Rose accompanies the Chief of Staff US Army, General Collins.

Jocks attend a concert party on a Korean hillside. Beyond was a 25-pounder gun line. When they fired the spectators could see the muzzle flashes but the cast could not and were horrified when the shells passed overhead – much to the amusement of the jocks.

In November 1952 the Battalion took over probably the most vital feature of the whole front from US Marines who had been suffering heavy attacks from the Chinese. This was the 'Hook'. From constant bombardment the position had been devastated so the Battalion set to work to dig and dig, constructing a whole new defensive position of dugouts and interconnecting tunnels. Corporal Strachan's Section from 'B' Company are building a 'hutchie' on the rear of the Hook. These provided protected living accommodation.

This view from a completed firing position is from 'C' Company's area looking from the Hook forward onto the 'Ronson' feature in no man's land. It was a spur leading onto the position which had to be covered by a permanent standing patrol which was changed every twenty-four hours.

In order to prevent the Chinese infiltrating onto the forward positions in the dark, patrols were sent out regularly and often had close contact with those of the enemy. Here, a fighting patrol from 9 Platoon is pictured dressed and armed ready for their mission.

There were to be two separate battles on the Hook for the Battalion. In both cases the position was held successfully but on the night of 18-19 November it was quite a close-run affair. Preceded by heavy artillery fire, the Chinese attacked in massed hordes. Eventually they were driven off by resorting to firing artillery airbursts on the position itself and by counter attacks. Major (later Brigadier) Angus Irwin is pictured outside his 'A' Company command post. He was awarded the Distinguished Service Order for his part in the battle having previously won the Military Cross at St Valery in 1940.

On Sunday 12 July 1953, on the day before the Battalion left Korea, a memorial service was held in Pusan for the fifty-seven officers and men of the Battalion who had died in the conflict and would not be returning home. The service was taken by the Padre, The Reverend Tom Nicol who was commissioned in the Regiment in 1940. After ordination he was the much loved padre of the 5th Battalion in North Africa and north west Europe and was awarded the Military Cross for recovering wounded under fire. On the left is the Commanding Officer, Lieutenant Colonel David Rose.

When the 1st Battalion sailed from Korea it went directly to another operational area, to Kenya which was then in the throes of the Mau Mau insurgency. The Battalion moved by train to Nairobi giving the jocks their first view of the countryside. After some familiarization training into a very different type of operation from those they had come from in Korea, the companies moved up into the Aberdare Mountains.

On Christmas Eve of 1953 Major The Earl Wavell was killed in action in Kenya less than four years after his father died. He was one of only six men of the Regiment who died during the operations in Kenya. His tragic death concluded a long line of distinguished soldiers and the third generation to serve in The Black Watch. Twice he had served under his father, first when the latter was Commander-in-Chief in Palestine and then in India and Burma when he was Viceroy. On both occasions he had been wounded, the second time was in 1944 when he was awarded the Military Cross.

Companies of the Battalion were dispersed in the Aberdares principally involved in carrying out patrols within the 'prohibited area' of the Forest, setting ambushes on the routes leading to and from it and conducting cordons and searches within the Kikuyu Reserve. Telephone lines were much used at one stage although eventually the terrorists took to cutting them and radios had to be relied on more heavily for communications. This line party is using a pony to carry the many miles of cable required.

In the dry season vehicular transport could be used on the tracks within the Aberdares. With eight men on board this patrol from 12 Platoon of 'D' Company reached the snowline on Mount Kenya. They are Privates Swinburne, King, Nolan, Robertson 07, Burke 48, Lance Corporals Bancroft and Kemp and 2nd Lieutenant Daldy.

The Military Band had not been deployed to Korea but rejoined the Battalion in Kenya where it was generally employed on musical duties around Nairobi. Meanwhile this rather impromptu group known as 'The Black Watch Mountain Band' played in company locations. They are Staff Sergeant Crabtree of the RAPC on the piano, Private Strachan, Private Murray on the drums, Corporal McAlpine and Colour Sergeant Grey.

Home at last! After almost three years abroad on active service in both Korea and Kenya, the 1st Battalion reached Glasgow aboard the troopship 'Empire Halladale' on 27 April 1955. During this period more than 3,000 officers and men had passed through the ranks of the Battalion – most of them National Service conscripts. Over 300 had become casualties and only sixty-nine had completed the full tour.

Eight
From 1954 to 1974

The twenty years from 1954 saw a substantial reduction in the size of the armed forces and, sadly, in The Black Watch too. From 1956 there was to be only one regular battalion. The two Territorial battalions survived longer intact but were also to be reduced in 1967. However, in September 1960 no more daunted by the weather than their Colonel-in-Chief, the 4/5th Battalion looms up out of the mist above Loch Muick on their march from Cortachy to Her Majesty's Deeside residence at Birkhall.

Less than four years after it had been amalgamated with the 1st Battalion, the 2nd was re-formed in April 1952 at a time when it became apparent that the Army needed to expand to cope with the demands of the Korean War. After a tour in Germany, it was posted to British Guiana. The salute at this Queen's Birthday Parade in Georgetown is being taken by the Governor, Sir Patrick Renison. Leading the company past the saluting base is Major (later Brigadier) Mike Wingate-Gray, who was later to command the SAS. Behind him is Lieutenant (later Brigadier) Thomas McMicking, whose father was the Colonel of The Regiment at the time.

National Servicemen were required to carry out an annual camp with the Territorial Army as part of their compulsory service after completing time in a regular unit. Camp was thus a very busy and vibrant time for the Territorial battalions. In July 1954 the 4/5th Battalion held its camp at Stobs, near Hawick. The Battalion is formed up ready to march to the railway station at the end of camp to entrain for Dundee.

On return from Korea the 1st Battalion was to be stationed at Crail only for less than a year but during this time it had the honour of providing the Royal Guard at Ballater. This was the seventh occasion on which the Regiment had done so. Her Majesty The Queen inspects the Guard of Honour on arrival at Ballater Station on 13 August 1955. She is accompanied by the Guard Commander Major (later Brigadier) Tony Lithgow who would command the Battalion in 1964 as would his son in 1990.

In 1956 the 1st Battalion moved to Berlin while the 2nd returned to Scotland from British Guiana where, after its short four year reprieve, it was disbanded. The jocks of the 1st Battalion posing at the Brandenburg Gate are Lance Corporals James Davidson and Albert Whittle and Privates Thomas McKenzie and Alexander Page.

The competence and standard of leadership of non commissioned officers is crucial to an efficient battalion and their selection and training has always had the highest of priorities in the Regiment. Using his pace stick to perfect the drill of the NCO cadre in Berlin is the Regimental Sergeant Major George Patterson. He had had a highly successful tour as Company Sergeant Major of 'A' Company throughout the operations in Korea and Kenya and would obtain a Quartermaster Commission in 1964. On his left is Private Jock Robb who also gained a commission in the Royal Pioneer Corps. Beyond him is Private (later Sergeant) 'Black' Beveridge, Privates Robson and Maxwell, and, behind, the RSM, Privates Wilson, Chalmers and Mitchell.

After Berlin the Battalion spent a year in Edinburgh before deploying to Cyprus in December 1958 towards the end of the EOKA emergency. Isolated detachments and observation posts in the Troodos Mountains had to be resupplied by carrying parties or helicopters. The donkey train is being lead by Private McCarthy followed by Privates Steadman and Quin.

With the emergency in Cyprus over, the Battalion moved into barracks in Dhekelia and to a more routine peacetime existence. Men of 'B' Company are being fitted with the tropical No.3 Dress before taking part in the final Guard at Government House before the independence of the island. Watching are the Quartermaster, Alan Glass, Captain William Dudgeon and Colin Harrison who was later to receive a Late Entry Commission.

Archbishop Makarios, the newly elected President of the Republic of Cyprus, made his first official visit to the Sovereign Base Area of Episkopi in late 1960. The Guard of Honour is formed by 'A' Company. Captain (later Major) Campbell Parker accompanies the Archbishop who had played a prominent part in the movement to break the connection with Britain. The Archbishop is passing 2nd Lieutenant Johnnie Henderson.

The year 1961 saw two changes to the Regiment. The move from Queen's Barracks was permanent. Fortunately, the other change was less so and the introduction of the Highland Brigade Cap Badge was relatively short-lived. With the end of National Service and the much smaller intake of recruits, it was decided that their training should be done on a more centralized basis. Initially it was planned that this should take place at Bridge of Don but later it was to be further centralized on a Scottish Divisional basis at Glencorse, near Edinburgh. The Regimental Headquarters moved to Balhousie Castle close by, in Perth. The final recruit squad passed out from Queen's Barracks on 11 March 1961.

After locking the gates of Queen's Barracks for the last time Major (Quartermaster) Nobby Clark hands over the keys on 31 May 1961. It is impossible to even try to estimate how many trained recruits had passed through those gates on their way to join battalions of the Regiment and to see action in the Sudan, in South Africa, in both world wars and in Korea. Major Clark himself had passed through them thirty-two years previously in 1929 and was to go on serving the Regiment for a further twenty-three years, until he retired as Secretary of the Black Watch Association. As for the watchman to whom the keys are being handed over – he is another Black Watch stalwart, ex-Company Sergeant Major 'Big Mac' McGregor. When the kilt was withdrawn at the start of the Second World War, the reason given was that it would prevent the Regiment being identified. It was Big Mac who made the oft repeated comment 'But damn it we *want* to be identified.'

In 1962 after return from Cyprus, the 1st Battalion took over the role of Demonstration Battalion at the School of Infantry, Warminster, a task which involved more than mere demonstrations including the development of new equipment and of minor tactics. This posed recruiting photograph shows Private Anderson 45 equipped with the 7.62mm Self-Loading Rifle raising a restraining hand before his section launches an assault.

To mark Her Majesty Queen Elizabeth The Queen Mother's 25th anniversary as Colonel-in-Chief, a parade of all three battalions of The Black Watch was held on the North Inch, Perth in September 1962. Accompanied by the Colonel of the Regiment, Major General The Viscount of Arbuthnott, she inspects the parade from a landrover. In the distance is the 4/5th Battalion, in the centre the 1st Battalion and, nearest the camera, the 6/7th Battalion. The 6/7th Queen's Colour is being carried by Lieutenant J.F. Rankin, the Regimental Colour by Lieutenant (later Sir Michael) Nairn and the Warrant Officer is Company Sergeant Major Beck.

Since their first tour in 1958, the Pipes and Drums have carried out fairly regular band tours of North America. The earlier ones were all accompanied by the Regimental Band but more recently the military band component of the tour has had to come from elsewhere. Pipe Major James Anderson is seen here instructing his pipers in the music for a forthcoming tour in 1963. A man of huge proportions, Anderson was Pipe Major of the 1st Battalion for a total of sixteen and a half years.

During the 1963 Band Tour of North America, President John F. Kennedy expressed a wish to be 'serenaded by The Black Watch'. This was duly arranged and, on 13 November the Pipes and Drums, Regimental Band and Dancers gave a performance on the South Lawn of the White House. Before they played, the President spoke to the invited audience after which he was presented with a Regimental dirk by Major (later Brigadier) Mike Wingate-Gray. In the photograph the dirk is being held by Piper Byrne and on the right is Mrs Jacqueline Kennedy. Nine days later President Kennedy was assassinated. By the special request of Mrs Kennedy, the Pipe Major and eight pipers led the President's funeral cortege from The White House to Washington Cathedral.

In February 1964 one platoon was detached from the 1st Battalion for a tour of duty in Cyprus. There, for the first time, soldiers of the Regiment wore the blue beret and United Nations badge as part of that organization's force holding the line between Greek and Turkish enclaves. Three years later the entire Battalion would be deployed on this task. The request to be allowed to wear the red hackle in the blue beret had been turned down but the platoon were permitted to place a tartan patch behind the UN badge. This group consists of Private Rooney, Corporal Wylie, 2nd Lieutenant (later Major) Paul Sugden and Sergeant (later Major) Bob Ritchie.

Later in 1964 the 1st Battalion moved from Warminster to Minden in what was then West Germany. There it was equipped with the Armoured Fighting Vehicle 432. This Armoured Personnel Carrier had only recently been introduced into service and the Battalion was tasked with developing techniques for making use of its floatation capability to cross water obstacles. These trials were carried out on the River Weser by 'D' Company. Major Alec MacDonald-Gaunt, the Company Commander, is in the cupola of this suitably numbered vehicle. The driver is Private Alfie Kitson and, on the back, is the signals Lance Corporal (later Major) Ronnie Proctor. He was to be Regimental Sergeant Major when the Battalion next undertook a tour of duty in Germany sixteen years later, was Quartermaster and is now Assistant Regimental Secretary.

Periodically the Battalion had to furnish patrols along the Inner German Border where the Communists had created a fearsome barrier of barbed wire, mines and machine guns to prevent escapes to the West. While such patrols may have done little to reassure the West Germans living near the Border they certainly made members of the Battalion realize why they were stationed in Germany. On the left of the picture are two West German Border Police then Sergeant Graydon and in the centre one of the British border controllers. Amongst the members of the patrol fifth from the right is Lieutenant (later Captain) Tom Brodie. No unit identification was permitted on these patrols hence the wearing of 'cap comforters'.

For long there has been a strong link between the Regiment and the Church of Scotland. The move to formalize this was a protracted process but eventually in 1953 the General Assembly authorized the 1st Battalion to form a properly constituted Kirk Session – the first in the British Army with the Elders drawn from all ranks and more recently wives as well. Visits from the Moderator of the General Assembly have been regular events. The Moderator in 1966 was Dr Wall seen here in his traditional dress with members of the Kirk Session – Major (later Colonel) The Hon David Arbuthnott, Captain (later Major) Duff Henderson, Lance Corporal Arthur Barty (since leaving the Army one of the Colonel-in-Chief's chauffeurs), the Padre Donald Beaton, Orderly Room Quartermaster Sergeant (later Major) Alan McKinnell, the Reverend Tom Nicoll, who had been the Battalion Padre in Korea and that of the 5th Battalion during the war, and Corporal Andy Hamilton.

From Germany the Battalion deployed on exercise to Libya to undertake the sort of mobile training which could not be carried out within the confines of German training areas. While there, opportunity was taken to visit Tobruk, scene of the 2nd Battalion's heroic action in 1941. Private (later Sergeant Major) Bruce Low admires the memorial on the battlefield. The memorial has since had to be moved to a new location.

Over the winter of 1966-1967 the Battalion donned the blue bonnet of the United Nations and was committed to a six-month tour of duty in Cyprus. Although there were one or two potentially serious confrontations, for the most part the task was one of showing the UN presence by patrolling and of observation to provide early warning of trouble. Typical of the many observation points manned by the Battalion is this one with Private Byrne on duty.

A further year was spent in Germany after the United Nations tour in Cyprus before the Battalion moved on to Kirknewton, west of Edinburgh. From there, 'B' Company undertook a chemical warfare exercise with Canadian forces on the prairies. For this, the establishment at Porton Down specially adapted a respirator for piping. While quite unrecognizable, this unique piece of equipment is in fact being used by Piper Scott.

From Kirknewton the Battalion also made a nine-month foray to Gibraltar as a reinforcement to the garrison at a time when there was more than usual dispute with the Spanish over the sovereignty. In December 1966, the Pipes and Drums and Military Band held a tattoo in St Michael's Cave, deep within the 'Rock'. Members of the Pipes and Drums performed the Argyll Broadswords. On the right is Corporal Paterson, a drummer, the other two visible in the photograph are pipers – the one facing being Private Mair.

In May 1740 the Regiment first paraded beside the Tay near Aberfeldy. In 1887 a monument was erected to commemorate the event. Two hundred and thirty years after the initial embodiment, the Regiment was granted the Freedom of the Burgh of Aberfeldy in September 1970. Afterwards those on parade, regulars, territorials, cadets and old comrades marched past the Provost and Colonel of The Regiment. The 1st Battalion Regimental Colour is being carried by Lieutenant (later Brigadier) Donald Wilson. The escorts are Sergeants Cathro and Holderness.

The year 1970 also saw the first of many deployments to Northern Ireland. The short sea passage from Scotland made the Battalion readily available for rapid reinforcement of the Province. Twice it went there that year and twice again in 1971. During the early stages of the troubles riot control was the main commitment though soon bombings and shootings would become all too prevalent. Here in Armagh, Lance Corporal Hay and Privates Cowie and Percival practice debussing armed with the unsophisticated weaponry and protection then available.

Another image of the first years deploying in Northern Ireland and of the lamentable conditions under which the jocks were often required to live. 'A' Company were based in the Short Strand Bus Depot in East Belfast. There, old buses provided basic, albeit cramped, cover within which to erect camp beds.

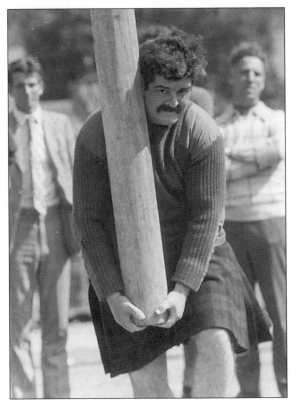

A far cry from the streets of Belfast; the Battalion was posted to Hong Kong in January 1972. There it was able to indulge in the full range of sporting activities which the Colony then provided. Yet the traditional sports of the Highland Games were not overlooked. Lance Corporal Ian Hunter is seen make a brave attempt to toss the caber ... it is not recorded whether he was successful.

After torrential rain in July 1972 there were serious landslides in Hong Kong, one of which engulfed a squatter settlement in the San Mau Ping area. From religious scruples the Chinese would not assist in the recovery effort. They can be seen watching in large numbers from the adjacent blocks while the jocks dig for victims of the disaster.

Hong Kong proved to be an excellent base from which to carry out training exercises in other parts of the Far East, Fiji, New Zealand, Australia and Korea. While in Fiji, 'D'Company took part in a joint parade with the Royal Fiji Military Forces on the occasion of the Queen's Birthday 1973. Very recently recruits from Fiji have joined the British Army and some are destined to serve with The Black Watch.

During 1973 'A' Company undertook a field training exercise in New Zealand and were visited by the Colonel of The Regiment at Waiowra. Lord Ballantrae had been Governor-General and Commander-in-Chief of New Zealand until five years previously. As Bernard Fergusson, he had been commissioned into the Regiment in 1931 and had served on both Chindit Expeditions during the war. He commanded the 1st Battalion in 1948. Beside him is the Company Commander, Major Colin Innes whose father, Berowald, had commanded the Battalion immediately prior to Bernard.

Besides providing several Korean Honour Guards in Seoul, a party of Korean veterans still serving with the 1st Battalion in Hong Kong paid their respects to their fallen comrades at the memorial in Pusan. Captain Hugh Rose nearest the camera was not in Korea but his father commanded the Battalion there. Next to him is Private Nobby Clark, then Corporal 'Spud' Thompson, Colour Sergeant Dave Anderson, Warrant Officer II Peter Herd and Warrant Officer II (later Captain) Colin Harrison.

Nine
From 1974 to 1999

The Pipes and Drums are the very heart of a Highland regiment for they epitomize the essential character, the music, the dress and traditions which make these regiments different and so very special. Suitably for the start of the final section covering the end of the twentieth century, the Pipe and Drum Majors of the Regiment are pictured on the steps of the Scottish National War Memorial, a memorial to those who died in the two world wars and in action since 1939. Photographed in 1993, they are from left to right: Drum Major D. Stark of the Territorial Battalion (but previously of the 1st Battalion), Pipe Major P.N. Snaddon of the Territorial Battalion, Pipe Major (later Regimental Sergeant Major) A. Brown of the 1st Battalion, Warrant Officer I.J.C. Rafferty, previously Pipe Major of the 1st Battalion then instructor at the Army School of Bagpipe Music, Drum Major A. Macpherson, 1st Battalion, Pipe Major (later Company Sergeant Major) S. Small and Drum Major P. Robson, both serving with the Army Training Regiment at Glencorse.

In May 1975, whilst the Battalion was stationed in Colchester, the Colonel-in-Chief presented new Colours. The Commanding Officer, Lieutenant Colonel (later Brigadier) Thomas McMicking elected to command the parade mounted and is seen passing the saluting dais where Her Majesty is accompanied by the Colonel of the Regiment, Brigadier J.C. Monteith. The Adjutant follows also mounted and is Captain (later Brigadier) Donald Wilson.

Operations in Northern Ireland occupied much of the Battalion's time throughout the 1970s and 1980s, but none so much as during 1976 and 1977, when it was the Province Reserve Battalion stationed at Ballykinler, Co. Down. From there, companies were deployed to trouble spots across Ulster, often at short notice. During this period many thousands of vehicles were stopped and searched to prevent the movement of arms and explosives. This road-block by men of 'A' Company is typical of the random checks conducted day and night throughout the year.

Keady Police Station in Armagh and the commander of a mobile patrol confirms the route before departure. The landrover has an armoured (macrolon) top cover with a hatch so that one of the patrol can ride 'shotgun' ready to return fire if necessary. The angle iron bar attached to the vehicle protects him from wires stretched across the road. There are also mesh covers for the lights and windows, those for the windscreen are in the lowered position. The jocks are wearing armoured 'flak' jackets.

While the troubles in Ulster kept on changing their pattern, urban rioting remained a perennial element amongst them. Here a mob attacks the heavily-protected Springfield Road Police Station in West Belfast. The platoon commander observes from behind cover while his platoon sergeant runs the gauntlet of missiles on some mission. He is armed both with rifle and the Federal Riot Gun, used to fire plastic bullets.

Once the Province Reserve task in Northern Ireland was completed the Battalion moved to Catterick from where it provided the 1978 Royal Guard. Since the closure of the railway to Ballater the Guards of Honour, on arrival, have been held at Balmoral Castle gates. It is there that Her Majesty is seen in animated conversation with the Guard Commander, Major (later Lieutenant Colonel) Stephen Lindsay, the Regimental Secretary. At the right of the front rank is the Company Sergeant Major (later Lieutenant Colonel) Mike Smith.

The tour in Catterick was broken by an operational deployment to Belize in 1979. A patrol passes through the ancient Mayan ruins of Xuantanich close to the border with Guatemala. It is led by Pipe Major Alan Dippie and consists of members of his platoon demonstrating that the Pipes and Drums are a fully-trained rifle platoon as well as a band.

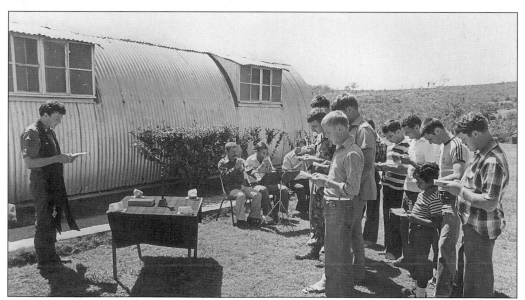

As the Battalion was spread between a number of bases in Belize, each Sunday the Padre would visit these accompanied by three members of the Regimental Band to conduct services. Here the Reverend Norman Drummond takes one for the Mortar Platoon with nearest the camera Corporal (later Sergeant) Mitchell and Sergeant (later Warrant Officer II) Bailey ... and the young lad between them is a local, honorary member of the Platoon.

The Werl Shutzenfest 1980 and the Military Band marches through the town, almost on home territory, for the Battalion moved there from Catterick and was in due course to be honoured with the Freedom of the town. The Band was largely instrumental in building such a close rapport with the local population. The Bandmaster is Norman Rogerson.

For infantry soldiers life in an Armoured Personnel Carrier equipped battalion adds many complexities and much additional responsibility for the non-commissioned officers in checking and maintaining items of equipment. During this inspection on the vehicle park in Werl, Lance Corporal McEwan checks his vehicle kit with Private Campbell.

When the Battalion had been in Germany, fifteen years before, mechanized field firing training was undertaken in Libya. With the change of regime in that country this was no longer possible and was now carried out in Canada. After leaving their vehicles in cover behind them, the platoon commander awaits the signal to assault and the piper to play the 'charge': Lieutenant (later Captain) Peter Burnet, Private McGowan and Private Cook.

The ice was two inches thick when this armoured carrier became bogged during driver training. Someone had to attach the tow rope to the front of the vehicle. One assumes the 'volunteer' was the unfortunate trainee driver at the time that it stuck.

'Jock and the Beanstalk'. Family entertainment has always played a part in a family regiment like The Black Watch. The production of this pantomime was a highlight of the 1982 Calendar in Werl with each company putting on a skit. The Families Officer, Captain Colin Harrison took on the part of Snow White with great aplomb.

Even the busy mechanized training season in West Germany had to be interrupted for emergency tours in Northern Ireland. The Battalion undertook one such tour in Belfast during the winter of 1982-1983. A jock takes cover in the doorway of Hynes Bar in the notorious Falls Road.

Soltau Training Area in Germany was the scene for a major chemical warfare trial which the Battalion undertook in the heat of the summer of 1983. As well as assessing the degradation in performance of soldiers operating for long periods in protective clothing, it emphasized the problems of recognition in this dress. Only the Regimental Sergeant Major (later Major) Ronnie Proctor is easily identifiable with his protectively coated pace stick. For the record the other two are the Second in Command, Major (later Lieutenant Colonel) Philip Halford-Macleod and the Commanding Officer, Lieutenant Colonel (later Brigadier) Edward de Broë-Ferguson.

From Germany the Battalion returned to Scotland in 1985 again to be stationed at Kirknewton. Later that year it undertook a tour of duty in South Armagh, a very different type of environment from its previous visit to Northern Ireland when it had been in Belfast. Travel by road in this rural area close to the border with the Republic was not safe, so patrols were carried out on foot and deployed and recovered by helicopter. Flying became a daily part of the jock's existence as in the case of these men from 'D' Company being airlifted to Crossmaglen.

In 1986 the Colonel-in-Chief presented new Colours to the Territorial Battalion, the 1st Battalion 51st Highland Volunteers. The historic Colours of the 6th Battalion were then laid up in the Regimental Museum in Balhousie Castle. These Colours had the distinction of being the oldest colours in service at the time – for they had been presented before the First World War. They are unique within the Regiment in bearing the Croix de Guerre awarded to the 6th Battalion in July 1918 when fighting in support of the French, near Rheims. The two Black Watch Territorial companies are formed up in the Wavell Garden before the Colours were handed over to the Regimental Secretary.

The XIII Commonwealth Games were held in Edinburgh in 1986 and for these the 1st Battalion was tasked to provide the manpower for all the ceremonial events from opening and closing ceremonies to the presentation of 487 medals. This party was responsible for the raising of the Commonwealth Games Flag at the Meadowbank Stadium.

After a gap of thirty years, the Battalion returned to Berlin in 1987. Although it was not to remain so much longer, the threat from the Warsaw Pact was still very real. Training for fighting in an urban setting was taken particularly seriously and much use made of the Ruhleben Fighting Village. Preparing to assault a building in it is, on the right armed with a General Purpose Machine Gun, Private Adamson, Private Holdsworth with a rifle and Pipe Major Joe Rafferty ready to play them in.

The annual British Military Tattoo in Berlin used to be a spectacular affair and with two Scottish battalions stationed there in 1988 the whole event was given a special 'Scottish' theme. Surrounded by jocks bearing flaming torches there was a spot in the programme for Scottish dancing. The Regimental dancers are those doing the country dances with the girls in sets around the arena.

The importance given to training potential non-commissioned officers has already been stressed. This photograph shows a different aspect of the same process, developing leadership and testing ingenuity – and of course one can always learn by one's mistakes! It is Private Nelson who looks as if he is trying to walk on water.

From Berlin it was back to Ballykinler for another accompanied tour in Northern Ireland. There, in May 1990, the 250th anniversary of the raising of the Regiment was marked by a battalion parade – albeit a depleted battalion as 'A' Company and other detachments were deployed on operational tasks. The Battalion Second-in-Command, Major (later Colonel) David Thornycroft leads the Battalion towards the saluting dais followed by Regimental Sergeant Major (later Captain) Brian Dickson, and 'B' Company Commander, Major (later Lieutenant Colonel) Ronnie Bradford.

With the Mountains of Mourne as a backdrop, the Battalion Dog Section stand with their charges in Ballykinler where they had responsibilities for security of the base. They are Privates Fieldston, Grover, Mackin and Lewis.

There are many photographs in this collection of ceremonial parades and there are more to come but this one was taken 'behind the scenes'. It shows the normal preparations by senior non-commissioned officers to ensure that the jocks are well turned out. This is 1991 when the Battalion had moved to Tern Hill and carrying out the inspection before a Regimental Sergeant Major's Parade are Company Sergeant Major Ross and Colour Sergeant Bell.

'Red Hackle Day' is the Regiment's annual celebration of the adoption of the 'Hackle' in 1795. Normally held on 5 January, it takes the form of a number of traditional events starting with tea laced with alcohol being served to the jocks in their billets to amongst others a fancy dress football match between the officers and senior non-commissioned officers. The Quartermaster, Captain (later Major) Jimmy Williamson, in the striped shirt, prepares to assist an unidentified officer being scragged by some of the opposition.

In its last few years as a colony, Hong Kong was to play a prominent part in the life of the Regiment. The 1st Battalion was to be the last British battalion stationed there when it left at the end of a two-year tour in 1994 – but was to return briefly in 1997 for the final handover to the Chinese. The principal task during the first of these visits was one of supporting the police in watching over the border and in anti-smuggling operations. Here, in one of the six observation posts manned along the border, Privates Mathieson and Brown 05 with Corporal Smith watch for activity by the Chinese Peoples Liberation Army.

Dragon Boat Racing is almost synonymous with Hong Kong but is becoming ever more popular elsewhere. The Battalion joined in the Tuen Ng Festival with enthusiasm, entering three teams, the 'Forty Twa', the 'Royal Highlanders' and the wives 'Black Watch Belles'. The twenty-four-man crew of the 'Royal Highlanders' are triumphant if exhausted after winning the semi-final.

It has long been an army tradition to take departing commanding officers out of barracks in style at the end of their tour. As a Chinese variation on the theme Lieutenant Colonel (later Colonel) Nigel Lithgow is given a ride in a rickshaw towed by the two Quartermasters: Captain (later Major) Jimmy Williamson and Captain (later Lieutenant Colonel) Mike Smith. It is interesting to note how the old pre-1881 regimental numbering still persists in the Battalion's memory with the mudguards marked 42 and 73.

The married families are very much an integral part of the Battalion, but this is perhaps not sufficiently apparent from this selection of photographs which concentrates on the more military side of the Regiment. Maybe this can be redressed by this delightful picture of Regimental children acting their nativity play in the Kirk of The Black Watch in Hong Kong, Christmas 1993. The wee shepherd on the right has even been made to look oriental.

After nearly 200 years' existence during which it made a huge contribution to the life of the Regiment in peace and in war, the Band of The Black Watch ceased to exist in April 1994 as part of the reductions in the size of the Army. Over the years it had provided music for parades, for route marches, for church services, for dinners, dances, concerts – and furthermore had gained enormous prestige for the Regiment from audiences it had played to around the world. Those in this final muster are, in the back row: A. Paterson, S. Brown, S. Grant, A. Dinning, D. Twycross, E. Gordon, G. Dodds and M. Innes. Seated are Corporals C. Goodhall, C. Meldrum, Sergeant R. Clark, Bandmaster I.R. Peaple, Band Sergeant J.S. Malcolm, Sergeant D. Clark and Corporal D. McMullan.

As was the case with the 1970s tour in Hong Kong, advantage was taken of every opportunity to train outside the Colony. This time Hawaii was added to the list of where exercises were held. There jocks of 'B' Company worked with US Marines and had the chance to display their daring, travelling on a suspended rope some 500ft above the sea.

From Hong Kong, the Battalion moved to Pirbright and, shortly afterwards, to the realities of life and yet another tour in Northern Ireland; Belfast once more during the summer of 1995. It was a town with a difference, for a ceasefire saw a much reduced military presence on the streets. However, the following year some of the Battalion were rushed to the Province as reinforcements at a time when Orange Order marches were causing trouble. The Mortar Platoon are pictured at the scene of an incident in Belfast.

On 24 September 1996 the Colonel-in-Chief presented new Colours to the 1st Battalion at her Deeside home, Birkhall, replacing those she presented in Colchester in 1975. The old Colours are marched off parade past Her Majesty. The ensigns are Lieutenant Stephen Cole and Lieutenant Anthony Fraser. The Colonel of the Regiment, Brigadier Garry Barnett, stands beside the Colonel-in-Chief and the Equerry, Major David McMicking behind.

The Presentation of Colours was followed by lunch in the summerhouse. Rather than drive back to the house afterwards, Her Majesty spontaneously decided to walk with the members of the Regiment. This lovely photograph shows the group making its informal return to Birkhall.

As the 2nd Battalion had done in Pakistan in 1948, and as the 1st Battalion had in 1960 in Cyprus, the Battalion was to play its part in the handover of part of the Empire – in this case Hong Kong, the last significant part of it. The first half of 1997 was devoted to this, a task which gradually changed from the physical emptying and handover of the few remaining camps to the ceremonial aspects of the final parade. Eventually, there was just one base left – Stonecutters Island. There, despite the language difficulties, the officers entertained those of the People's Liberation Army when this rather unique group photograph was taken. In the front is the Commanding Officer, Lieutenant Colonel Alasdair Loudon and the Second-in-Command, Major (later Lieutenant Colonel) Mike Riddell-Webster.

The final withdrawal from Empire is symbolized in the photograph of the Farewell Parade in Hong Kong on 30 June 1997. The Colours are marched off in an ever-increasing downpour. The Colour ensigns are Nick Ord and Angus Bushby, Sergeant Major Gilfillan and Colour Sergeants Anderson and Baxter.

A scene witnessed by many millions of people around the world, that of Pipe Major Steven Small playing a lament in the torrential rain which marked the end of British control of Hong Kong.